VOLUNTEERING:
THE SELFISH BENEFITS

How to Achieve

Deep-Down Satisfaction

and Create That Desire in Others

"America was built into the greatest country the world has ever known, not through government control, regulation and handouts; but rather through individual imagination and initiative. It has been the individual and not government that built this nation, and it will be the individual that will save it for future generations."
—ROBERT W. MILLER, PRESIDENT, FREEDOMS FOUNDATION

VOLUNTEERING:
THE SELFISH BENEFITS

How to Achieve

Deep-Down Satisfaction

and Create That Desire in Others

CHARLES A. BENNETT

First printing, September 2001

Published in the United States of America by
Committee Communications, Inc.
P. O. Box 343 Oak View, CA 93022

Library of Congress Control Number: 2001 130652

Publisher's Cataloging-in-Publication Data

Bennett, Charles A.
    Volunteering: The Selfish Benefits
    Ojai, California: Committee Communication, Inc. 2001

    Includes Index
    ISBN 0-9709324-0-5

DISCLAIMER

This book is designed to provide information helpful in volunteer activities. It is sold with the understanding that the publisher and author are not engaged in rendering legal, accounting or other professional service. If legal or other expert assistance is required, the services of a competent professional should be sought.

It is not the purpose of this manual to reprint all the information that is otherwise available to the author and/or publisher, but to complement, amplify or supplement other texts. You are urged to read other available material. Learn as much as possible about volunteering and leadership. Then tailor the information to your individual needs.

Every effort has been made to make this book as complete and as accurate as possible. However, there may be mistakes both typographical and in content. Therefore, this text should be used only as a general guide, not as the ultimate source of information about volunteering, volunteer leadership or the setting up and running of an organization.

The purpose of this manual is to educate and entertain. The author and Committee Communications, Inc. shall have neither liability nor responsibility to any person or entity with respect to any loss or damage caused, or alleged to be caused, directly or indirectly by the information contained in this book.

*This book is dedicated
to the individual and organizations
who demonstrate daily
what Americanism
is all about.*

"All who have meditated on the art of governing mankind have been convinced that the fate of empires depends on the education of youth. Educated men are as much superior to uneducated men as the living are to the dead."

—ARISTOTLE (384-322 B.C.)
GREEK PHILOSOPHER: PUPIL OF PLATO;
TUTOR OF ALEXANDER THE GREAT

CONTENTS

PREFACE

■ ■ ■ ■ ■ ■ ■ ■ ■ ■ ■ ■ ■ ■ ■ ■ ■ ■ ■

The most important reason to own this book is to expand your ability to be personally happy and satisfied. In the end, surveys find that those before us wished they had done more social good in this world with the precious few moments they had in this life. We hunger to be a complete human being. We all have that insatiable yearning to do more for society. Who ever said, "Life is tough—and then you die" may have flickered a macabre smile on our thought patterns. However it is the quality of every "tough" life which matters the most. The quality of our life is much more important than the quantity of years left. Quality of life is internal. This book is for the hard-working accomplishment oriented individual who knows that a ten percent improvement within ourselves can make all the quality difference. The difference from just "showing up," to being an inspiration to a whole group.

This volume will put the power and essence of who you are back in your hands. What you will discover can then be used for the betterment of all. The alarming, out-of-control problems of youth: youth education, young marriages, and drug use over the past 40 years should be proof enough that we cannot buy our way out of problems. Recent history is clear enough. Let us return to many of the

" We pass the word around; we ponder how the case is put by different people; we read the poetry; we meditate over the literature; we play the music; we change our minds; we reach an understanding. Society evolves this way, not by shouting each other down, but by the unique capacity of unique, individual human beings to comprehend each other. "
— LEWIS THOMAS (1913-1993), U.S. BIOLOGIST

proven methods of self-reliance and personal involvement this book is dedicated to.

If only a few more of us pick up the ideas and principles discussed here, there is no doubt we can change the world for the better. Ceasing hunger, war, or any serious problem is a function of communication beginning with the family and extending to community level. It is a steady and constant effort by each of us as individuals. When we stop, a bit of time goes by, a child grows up unaware of the learned rules—and the problems are renewed. Allow this situation to continue and soon you have a gang roaming the neighborhood. And then what?

Raising happy and productive families is the major legacy most of us leave. This book is for those who want to do that and more. It was written from the continuing belief that working together in smaller self inspired teams is the best way to get things done. Teams of motivated individuals accomplish so much more than simply attaining a goal. Successful teams fundamentally grow and develop people in a multitude of positive, synergistic ways.

While there is no escaping big business and big government, we as individuals must continue to do our part. We are here to play out our role, as worker, teacher, parent, psychologist, organizer and role model—every day, as best we can. The opportunity to achieve major improvements in your lifetime is here in your hands. The choice is yours.

—Charles A. Bennett, Ojai California, 2001

THE LOGIC AND PURPOSE
OF SELFISH VOLUNTEERING

You may already be involved in an organization and looking for more clues to a surer footing on the path that you are on. You want to make a difference, not just "show up." This is a step-by-step guide to help you get involved by working together toward collective goals which you are interested in and excited about.

After reading the first few chapters, feel free to jump around to what interests you at the moment. Take an idea and purposefully implement it. Perhaps it will be a better way to get along, or to motivate someone. It could be a self-improvement idea or a money making idea. Just one idea implemented into your life permanently—pays for this book. You are continually changing, not just reading and agreeing with what you see here. How to make it happen in real world time is accomplished in small degrees. Many of us have tried leaping for great change, in a short burst of energy, and fall back. Change, real change, may appear miniscule and irrelevant at the time, but when habit is established, there is real satisfaction. After one goal is accomplished choose another growth tool to work on. Most important—keep yourself aware of the change you desire. Keep at the goal until it is natural and innate.

The Benefits for You are Grouped:

Chapters One and Two: `WHY WE NEED YOU`

- **To see how a society works** we look at human nature and history. The ability to accomplish something worthwhile in your community, and in your life, comes through trust and integrity. This workbook will help you find the pulse. It will help you to be better attuned, to be prepared, up and aware, to give you the confidence to pick a goal in your community and know you will attain it. This book will give you practiced solutions to everyday problems which individuals, looking to improve, face all the time.

Chapter Three: `ABOUT YOUR HAPPINESS`

- **To help make you happier than you've been in years.** Deep-down happy. Establish in your mind that your first choice is truly what you want to do. Help you in establishing a personable working foundation. Develop a flexible, stretchable form of your own creation that you can feel comfortable working within to your heart's content.

Chapters Four and Five: `YOUR FOCUS`

- **How to make a social contribution by becoming self-actuated**. This book contains methods for gaining consensus with others, becoming more accomplished within your work, your volunteer organization, and your community. Here are solutions for you to more easily achieve ambitious goals with many suggestions to stay happily focused on a satisfying mission.

Chapter Ten: **YOUR LEGACY**

• **Finally, how will you be remembered?** Most older people say similar things when they reminisce. They say they would pause more often and reflect on the meaning of life rather than working so hard for work's sake. When you approach the second half of your life, everything seems to pick up speed. When we are old we don't want to say, "So what did it matter"?

#1. THE SELFISH BENEFITS OF VOLUNTEERING

IN THE FACE OF EVER INCREASING CHANGE—IT'S OUR GROUNDING

Bracing against a constant worldwide hurricane of information and opportunity, waste and confusion are the feelings many of us experience in the world of making a living. No matter when you pick this book up the news is going to be that change is towards us more and more rapidly. Those who suffer the most angst are often the least prepared. In hurricanes the flora and fauna with adequate shelter, foundation and root systems survive and indeed thrive afterwards. The good news is that the success tools for humans in this ever increasing roar are the further refinement and simplification of people skills which have been around since the human race began communicating.

As change continues its acceleration, the feedback is the same as it has always been. Effective organizations, teams and indeed families, result from the basic values of mutual support and nurturing.

It is the age-old truth of cause and effect. For every action there is a reaction. The faster the game is played the more trained the players must be while the ultimate goal is a score and the mission is winning all the time. The real work is how the players integrate, interact and work together. The faster the game accelerates the more important the basic interrelationships become.

Is this a hurricane or the universe that you are looking into? It may depend on how insignificant or secure you feel. It could be powdered cream being stirred in your coffee cup. Vast or small ideas; it is what you do with the possibilities that counts.

In nature we see this as well. In reality our spinning world is a marvelous example. Try to imagine a more complex situation. On one level a pin prick of an earth spinning rapidly on its axis and hurtling around an average size sun on the outskirts of the Milky Way. On another level, we live in the calm of all this activity. Literally, it is like living in the eye of a hurricane which is perfectly calm. What we see in nature is often perfectly calm in appearance and feeling.

When our planet becomes unbalanced and begins to wobble, and it is abundantly clear that it has a few times, is the cause a volcanic uproar from a major shift of the earth's crust? The effect from speed, gravity, orbit, an ice age? A resettling above and below the crust? Who knows? All life is tenuous. We deal with what we can learn about.

Resembling the physical universe similar pressures build over time, explode and resettle within civilizations. The more we can appease the potential for an explosive war, the better for us all. Knowledge gained and remembered at every level is why the study of history is so vital when planning future goals.

With the high level pace of team play and accomplishment, comes the need for greater understanding of basic key plays. The quicker the teams play or work, the more basic the understanding of the key plays must be. Long-lived trees survive hurricanes by having a great tap root or larger main roots reaching down into the earth. Trees with only surface roots get blown away in the storm. We as a people fare no differently. If we do not learn and comprehend many past truths, we become more easily disoriented and dysfunctional. The effect of media hype and public perception actually influences change that need not happen. These changes most often occur at the family level, frequently at the community level, sometimes at the state level and occasionally at the national level. In recent history, World Wars followed.

No matter how quickly you want to play the game of life, the basic process—the foundation must be there. First within you and then within your team. There is no

> *" People don't change very much. The trappings around them change—the society, the politicians, the governments—but people are essentially the same. We are a tribal species that seems fiercely loyal to our own, whether our own is our country or our particular race or religion or belief. "*
> —BRIAN STOKES MITCHELL

escaping this fundamental fact. The more rapidly you go the more basic and solid your foundation must be.

Whether you are with your sports team, an infantry army platoon, or even a country—in the whirling fury of a hurricane, you can't hear yourself shout. What is moving your team through to the goal? Integrity. Integrity comes from trust. They both come over time and through knowledge of each other. Integrity cannot be taught directly, it has to be earned. It is learned by example.

We can't change others. They must change on their own. It is part of their character. Each person must be his/her own witness to life. We learn when we are ready, not when others are ready to teach us. Teachers and leaders prepare for the question, that wonderful teaching moment. Great teachers anticipate and preset opportunities for learning.

Great coaches and great business leaders of great companies find those people who already have integrity. They make super teams by first finding the best building blocks. Where do these building blocks come from? They are individuals who come from positive and supportive backgrounds. Solid families, solid churches, solid organizations and support groups within those communities.

There is no "which came first the chicken or the egg?" in this scenario. Great governments or great businesses did not come first. Great individuals came first. Character matters more than self-esteem. Self-esteem evolves from character, not vice-versa. Our mission in a high paced lifestyle is to hold to the basics, our historical mores.

Alexis de Tocqueville was a french politician writing and traveling in America in 1831. His eloquent oft-quoted prose took awhile to become popular here since it was in French. He wrote about America's mores: about volunteerism, about self-help, about our sharing, about our willingness to take on individual responsibilities for big tasks. He was here when we were truly a melting pot of ideas, and nationalities. Character counted.

"It is their mores, then, that make the Americans of the United States capable of maintaining the rule of democracy; and it is mores again that make the various Anglo-American democracies more or less orderly and prosperous.

Europeans exaggerate the influence of geography on the lasting powers of democratic institutions. Too much importance is attached to laws and too little to mores. Unquestionably those are the three great influences which regulate and direct American democracy, but if they are to be classed in order, I should say that the contribution of physical causes is less than that of the laws, and that of laws less than mores.

I am convinced that the luckiest of geographical circumstances and the best of laws cannot maintain a constitution in despite of mores, whereas the latter can turn even the most unfavorable circumstances and the worst laws to advantage. The importance of mores is a universal truth to which study and experience continually bring us back. I find it occupies the central position in my thoughts; all my ideas come back to it in the end."
— *Alexis de Tocqueville (1805-59)*
French Statesman and Author

Let us discuss "then" versus "now" in America. How would Tocqueville express America's mores today? Are we apathetic? Or are we at an important part of the cycle of history (p. 15) that our collective ego has us pulling back from others and being more self-centered? We meet and visit with fewer and fewer people, become more and more opinionated on subjects that have a wide variety of answers. Like personal freedoms, war, and the environment.

Tocqueville said, "Nothing in my opinion is more deserving of our attention than the intellectual and moral associations of America." He continued, "in democratic countries, the science of association is the mother of science; the progress of all of the rest depends upon the progress it has made." How are our intellectual and moral associations progressing or regressing today?

Tocqueville also said, "When an association is allowed to establish centers of action at certain important points of the country, it's activities are increased and it's influence extended. Men have the opportunity of seeing one another face to face and the means of execution are combined. Opinions are maintained with a warmth and energy that written language can never attain.."

In his book, <u>Tocqueville Speaks</u>, Fred Caruso says:

"The individual's significance (personal power) and identity are diminished as governmental intervention in day-to-day life increases. Associations provide individuals with identity, special-interest communication and interaction (networking). Associations provide an opportunity for power in the necessary interface and interaction with the government.

Governmental intervention seems to grow in proportion to social democracy's growth, making government an integral part of every aspect of life. Therefore, the difference between civil and political associations virtually vanishes. Civil associations become political in nature and political associations become civil in nature.

Tocqueville very clearly stated, and few would dispute him today, that associations have more power than the press. Because of the tremendous diversity of interest of associations, it is doubtful that any one or two will have so much power as to be a threat to society. On the contrary, the many hundreds of thousands of small, special-interest associations have enough power in their own sphere of influence to significantly impact in a favorable way the people they serve.

Associations are a communications medium of high social value. They are important tools of modern life. Today's citizens must learn how to use them as vehicles for achieving their personal goals as well as the goals of our global society."

Americanism—Because of Volunteers

Let us get a larger picture concerning our reason to be here by reflecting upon the past few hundred years or even a century or two and look at the history of volunteers, sharing and associations. Historical science is the collection of facts. Science is information about material things. Indeed history shows us that anyone of us have far more of the material things and physical pleasures than did most kings back then.

The average old age was 46 up until 1900. Our age has almost doubled. It appears our need to pass the torch has smoldered to embers. It seems that twice the time to accomplish something results in half the effort overall. How very sad.

Who has had a happier more satisfactory life? Then, or now? If you could decide, how would you answer? Where does that deep down satisfaction come from? Would you cull out the scientific clutter, the material things in life as not being part of real fulfillment? What about the self-centered egoism so many people display through actions and "toys"? "I'm great. Other people aren't worth my effort!" The one critical arena then and now is knowledge. The ability to collect, absorb and pass along knowledge. A complete life comes from wholeness, a completeness, a universal experience. Historically you can believe these people thought that knowing it all was just as impossible as it is today. The difference today is that we have miles of data just listing places to look for information. We have huge, free information sources on the internet that makes us feel insignificant and overwhelmed by what is available to us.

Our biggest challenge today is to discover and explore deep down satisfaction. When we learn what is real for you and I, then we can discuss helping others. We must be properly grounded.

So, let us start with the self—you! How can you feel deep down satisfaction without comparisons? How good you can feel now probably depends on how bad you felt when you were young, gaining that knowledge.

A person in a bad auto accident will feel tremendous satisfaction just to be able to walk again. This is a very vertical low/high satisfaction slot in life experiences. Examples of narrow niches like this are all around us and are also called vertical markets. Typical jobs today are slotted even more in-depth in ever narrower specialty fields.

When we say the world is going faster, what are we really saying? New information is becoming more and more accessible. We can look very deeply into seemingly every slice of life. In fact, we seem to enjoy the fact that each of us specializes and may become highly paid consultants. Even the term generalist crosses only a few bands of these vertical markets. Are we improving? Are generalists of the old school being totally intimidated?

What did they have as a nation in 100 AD that we don't have now? Well, a number of very important things, mainly with reference to knowledge. Let's list some and compare self-satisfaction and associations—ancient history versus now.

Many under 50 do not have the general knowledge, or the general education to grasp a deep down satisfaction. Who remembers being forced to share? The wider the knowledge creates a more stable basis for life—less psychosis, paranoia, and the better balance for all concerned. The more interdependent, and forced to share we were, the better for a society and the individual. Everyone's world had to be wider. People were not easily put on TILT!

In 1948 Richard Weaver wrote the book <u>Ideas have Consequences</u> wherein he says;

> "It has been said countless times in this country that democracy cannot exist without education. The truth concealed in this observation is that only education can be depended on to bring men to see the hierarchy of values. That is another way of saying what has also been affirmed before, that democracy cannot exist without aristocracy.

> This aristocracy is a leadership which, if it is to endure,
> must be constantly recruited from democracy; hence it is
> equally true that aristocracy cannot exist without
> democracy. But what we have failed to provide against is
> the corruption of the system of recruitment by equalitarian
> dogma and the allurements of materialism."

How important is that? We have computer chat rooms where people discuss and rail at each other live by typing back and forth across continents online. Their input and reception is completely from words on a monitor. I have clients I do work for that I haven't seen face to face in years. Is that an advantage over the past? There are distinct advantages, but when it come to satisfaction—deep-down satisfaction, are there advantages? Part of personal satisfaction is approval through all the senses. Who's better off? Those who lived in the past or now?

Plato was concerned as to whether philosophy should be written down? Weaver again says Plato's conclusion was that, "philosophy exists best in discourse between persons, the truth leaping up between them like a flame."

Weaver, "In explanation of this important point he makes Socrates relate a myth about the Egyptian god Theuth, a mighty inventor, who carried his inventions before King Thamus desiring that they be made available to the people. Some of the inventions the King praised; but he stood firmly against that of writing, declaring that it could be only a means of propagating false knowledge and an encouragement to forgetfulness. Socrates adds the view that anyone who leaves writing behind on the supposition that it will be "intelligible or certain" or who believes that writing is better than knowledge presented to the mind is badly mistaken."

We have only to look at the current arguments over the interpretation of our written constitutional amendments, like free speech and gun control, to know that he was right. This becomes profound when you consider the importance of an association to collectively voice opinions of the individuals in it. It is the face-to-face discussions that make all the difference—that create all the excitement. Words on paper can begin the flame of an idea, or finish it off, but it will always be the group meeting face-to-face that gets the job done.

Getting Back in Touch with One Another

The goal is to recognize more clearly what you want out of life and how to work happily with others to attain individual desires for mutual gain.

As worldly communication speeds up so does our "quick view" daily media appear to concentrate more and more on the world stage. This is backward for future planning in a faster world. When holding our world as a sphere in your own two hands, let us remember what a speck it really is in the Supreme Being's grand scheme of things. Look for the speck of color on that globe that is your community. That is where our efforts are most effective. Certainly volunteer efforts. If just one more of us did a little bit more in our local community, imagine the impact it could have for the integrity of the planet? How can you and I have maximum influence and impact? How presumptuous of anyone to try to influence and impress others around the globe when we have no hands-on-knowledge of how they are living their lives. We see big enough mistakes with our own children.

"Real human progress depends upon a good conscience."
— ALBERT EINSTEIN (1879-1955) GERMAN-AMERICAN PHYSICIST

To have an impact somewhere else, we need to be there and see for ourselves. The most important responsible effort we could possibly do is still by example setting, one-to-one in our own community.

We should never have looked to "big brother" to oversee us. We make serious mistakes when we allow government or a business in a community to attempt to manage things. Neither institution should even donate money to the community. Large infusions of money and structure seem like the easiest and fastest way to solve problems. When it comes to long term success, they are not. Both government and business should encourage their employees to "get involved." Employees are the most important shareholders of their community. Think of the possibilities. If government were to lower taxes while business increased compensation. If companies offered some other incentive so their employees, participating as individuals, could contribute on their own.

Our solutions are the same as they always have been—it's people voluntarily helping people. The complaint is often that, "they don't contribute when asked." They don't understand the needs yet.

This is your community. You live here. This is you. It's about you. If you don't do anything here it's still about you. It has always been about you, even after you're dead.

> "Show me the manner in which a nation or a community cares for its dead and I will measure with mathematical exactness the tender sympathies of its people, their respect for the law of the land and their loyalty to high ideals."
> —Motto appearing on funeral-industry paraphernalia Quoted by Judith Newman in Harper's Magazine

■■■■■■■■■■■■■■■

HUMANITY IS LIKE THE OCEANS: CONSTANTLY RISING AND FALLING

All the chaotic pulling and pushing within and without keeps the apparent chaos of the sea in sync. Big and little fish are all inextricably linked, they feed off each other. Bill Gates wouldn't have his first dollar today if many little fish didn't want what he had to offer, or if he didn't see the benefit in helping smaller fish. What if there wasn't a rhythm? Even the way our heart beats and the way we breath are rhythms out of chaos constantly going on inside our bodies. It may be teamwork overall but it is also every little thing doing it's own job as best it can.

Countries and societies are constantly evolving through the same process. Historically, every country, community or organization goes through an ongoing life cycle. The new rhythm energy is always the result of great energy to pull together, usually under adverse conditions, all for the mutual good. Misunderstanding, argument and anarchy are present in the beginning too. Organization and structure follow as the entity becomes united in agreement and sophistication. Then the

66 Socialism works in two places; in heaven where it is not needed, and hell where they already have it. 99
—WINSTON CHURCHILL

hard fought for original "mission" becomes taken for granted and recedes into the background. More time is spent internalizing the needs, on reinforcing the structure of what we need every day. We worry more about each other than the policies that give us goals to keep a country, community or organization moving forward. We look internally instead of to the future. People want more from government. Bureaucracy increases. Volunteers do less, politicians and board members venture out less into their communities and make more and more laws and by-laws. Micro managing all things becomes an obsession as everyone vies for more shreds of control. Mission? What mission? " I'm too busy with what's important for me and my family. Let government take care of the rest." Then comes the fall, many times much too quickly, in a thundering crash of in-fighting and eye-gouging. This is how the Roman Empire and Russia fell and how most obsessively controlling countries fall eventually. As surely as people live and die, this cycle is repeated. Nobody wants to be part of the fall. Some see us at the brink already. I don't think so. Our government has made some well meaning, but serious mistakes. Our five trillion dollar "War Against Poverty" has only made things worse. Our American tradition of volunteerism was very seriously undermined. The federal welfare state has politicized the efforts of people-helping-people at the local level. "In 40 states, welfare pays more than an $8.00 per hour job. In 17 states the welfare package is more generous than a $10.00 per hour job"—Tanner, 1996.

In 1996 Congress passed the Welfare Reform Bill reversing 30 years of federal welfare expansion. "We've already seen a 30 percent to 40 percent decline in welfare case loads in many states."

—S. Moore, July 1998.

The Continuum of a Civilization

Dean Russell describes how nineteen of the world's greatest societies began and ended. None were destroyed by outside enemies, all fell from internal decay. The average age of these civilizations was about 200 years. With rare exception they all passed through Russell's sequence of conditions.

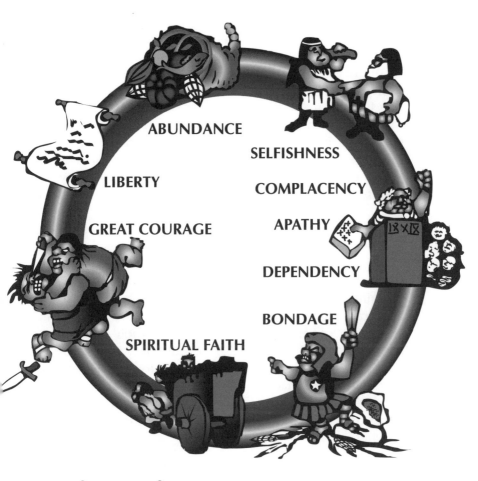

CONTINUUM OF A CIVILIZATION:

     From Bondage to Spiritual Faith
     From Spiritual Faith to Great Courage
     From Great Courage to Liberty
     From Liberty to Abundance
     From Abundance to Selfishness
     From Selfishness to Complacency
     From Complacency to Apathy
     From Apathy to Dependency
     From Dependency back to Bondage

—Dean Russell, A Short History of Liberty:
"How far along the way is America?"
The FREEMAN—June,1955

Where do you believe America now stands in that continuum cycle? Our continuum rhythms become like the pendulum causing the ticking of a grandfather clock. As the hours and minute hands take us ever progressively through our own societal continuum. Every swing of that pendulum can be likened to the energy of a generation. All our individual lifetime energies, like raising a family, completes a successful smaller and tighter swing within the larger societal swing of two hundred years on average. When perception causes us to overreact as a society, the continuum of the pendulum can be speeded up. We all clamber on to heave it forward. We think we know an easier way to a great societal improvement. The cycle is accelerated, the machinery gets off balance, we lose track. The more we collectively try to tinker with the machinery, (the natural course of things) the more off-balance the workings become. We think we are improving on what our forefathers set up, yet we don't have the painful personal experiences that underscored their reasoning at the beginning of the cycle. Let us put our trust back in one another. Allow each of us the opportunity to be interdependent to see that we must help each other in order to be successful ourselves. This is how we slow down the pace of a continuum and enjoy the richness of one another.

■■■■■■■■■■■■■■■■■■■

VOLUNTEERS CARRY THE VALUES OF AMERICAN SOCIETY

Volunteers carry on the American tradition. Volunteers are neither business nor government. Volunteers rarely produce a tangible product or enforce any regulation. Volunteering is what holds this country together. Volunteers are the gut mesentery of America! Volunteers are you and I. We come mostly from small communities in which lie business and government jobs. Our product is a re-charged human being. A volunteer's product is a "cured patient": a child who learns and improves: boys and girls who grow into self-respecting adults with character and integrity. We foster self-help, patriotism, comradeship and goodwill. Wow!

The book, Reclaiming America cites that about 62 percent of our population is not involved in any organization. Only 10 percent is involved in two or more. This may seem a sad statement: 10 percent of an average small town, or area of 7,000 population, is still 700 people actively involved in the community. Today much more can be done with much less.

It was volunteers, our immigrant ancestors, who wrote our constitution and fought and died to start this country. America is volunteers. We work together as a team. We cannot do it individually or by fiat.

The Price America's First Volunteers Paid

"Five signers were captured by the British as traitors, and tortured before they died. Twelve had their homes ransacked and burned. Two lost their sons in the revolutionary Army, another had two sons captured. Nine of the 56 fought and died from wounds or the hardships of the Revolutionary War.

What kind of men were they? Twenty-four were lawyers and jurists. Eleven were merchants, nine were farmers and large plantation owners, men of means, well educated. But they signed the Declaration of Independence knowing full well that the penalty would be death if they were captured.

They signed and they pledged their lives, their fortunes and their honor.

Carter Braxton of Virginia, a wealthy planter and trader, saw his ships swept from the seas by the British navy. He sold his home and properties to pay his debts and died in rags.

Thomas McKeam was so hounded by the British that he was forced to move his family almost constantly.

He served in the Congress without pay. His possessions were taken and poverty was his reward.

Vandals or soldiers or both, looted the properties of Ellery, Clymer, Hall, Walton, Gwinnett, Heyward, Ruttledge and Middleton.

At the Battle of Yorktown, Thomas Nelson, Jr., noted that the British General Cornwallis, had taken over the Nelson home for his headquarters. The owner quietly urged General George Washington to open fire, which was done. The home was destroyed, and Nelson died bankrupt.

Francis Lewis had his home and properties destroyed. The enemy jailed his wife, and she died within a few months.

John Hart was driven from his wife's bedside as she was dying. Their 13 children fled for their lives. His fields and his grist mill were laid to waste. For more than a year he lived in forests and caves, returning home after the war to find his wife dead and children vanished. A few weeks later he died from exhaustion and a broken heart.

Norris and Livingston suffered similar fates.

Such were the stories and sacrifices of the American Revolution These were not wild-eyed, rabble-rousing ruffians. They were soft-spoken men of means and education. They had security, but they valued liberty more. Standing tall, straight, and unwavering, they pledge: 'For support of this declaration, with a firm reliance on the protection of the Divine Providence, we mutually pledge to each other, our lives, our fortunes' and our sacred honor.'"

—Officer Review Magazine, 1997

> **"Yes, we did produce a near perfect Republic. But will they keep it, or will they, in the enjoyment of plenty, lose the memory of freedom? Material abundance without character is the surest way to destruction."**
> — THOMAS JEFFERSON (1743-1826) U.S. STATESMAN, ARCHITECT, AUTHOR AND THIRD PRESIDENT OF THE U.S.

Our country's founding volunteers cared very deeply when they shook hands. Their lives and their families' lives were on the line. That required trust and integrity few of us have ever witnessed or imagined.

Let us re-dust off our mission, our country's mission and our spiritual mission. Really, they are all the same.

> "Of course we look to the past for inspiration, but inspiration is not enough. We must have action. Action can only come from ourselves; society, government, the state, call it what you will, cannot act; our only strength, our only security, lies in the individual. American institutions are built on that foundation. That is the meaning of self-government, the worth and the responsibility of the individual. In that America has put all her trust. If that fail, democracy fails, freedom is a delusion, and slavery must prevail."
>
> —Calvin Coolidge

Leadership is by Our Example

When addressing the problems of our country and the world, the solution is not who should lead, or who should be our president, or king. What we need to address is the process that will constantly assure us that leadership will be there for us and from us. That leadership comes from people like us: that we still care enough for our fellow humans.

Our "Teamwork Challenge" has you, the reader, as the leader. The leader who is the necessary catalyst and mainstay to restart the process. This basic process has built and sustained the largest organizations on the planet. The desire here is for the average person to start and sustain a voluntary group that will accomplish significant things locally. What you will need to build, or rebuild your visionary organization, can be learned from this resource you hold in your hand.

Let's Create Solutions
—Enough of This Talk, Talk, Talk
About This Country Falling Apart

"I must admit that I personally measure success in terms of the contributions an individual makes to her or his fellow human beings."

— MARGARET MEAD
(1901-1978)
U.S. ANTHROPOLOGIST

Enough about families disintegrating, gangs increasing, or the drug war escalating. Like a messy office, bedroom, garage: in time we come to realize that efficiency and organization is easier.

In the end, who or what will have mattered? Making 50 businesses much more successful at selling widgets? Or getting in touch and changing the lives of 50 kids, or 50 adults in a business or in the community? Which will you remember most proudly on your death bed?

The saddest words said today, "I'm just one person. The problem is so big, why even try?"

#2: RECLAIMING AMERICA'S VISION A COMMUNITY AT A TIME

■■■■■■■■■■■■■■■■■■■■

To be loved, is to love. We feel successful only when we believe we've helped others to be successful. You and I are inextricably linked. I must help you up to get myself up.

Our community is you. You are part of our town. If none of us does anything—it's still us. Gaining understanding of our identity and what we want to personally be responsible for is what this chapter will discuss. Towns and communities, like governments, and nations are made up of people. The biggest mistake we make today is referring to larger entities as "they" and "them". 'They" and "them" is really "us": Tom, Mary, Maurice and Kim. Real people. Usually we think of "they" in higher levels of government as a large group. Most often it's two or three somewhat knowledgeable people that make a final decision. They are the government worker-bees. Think of the last time your relatives got together for a big reunion. Running a town is a lot like

" A good government implies two things; first, fidelity to the object of government, which is the happiness of the people; secondly, a knowledge of the means by which that object can be best attained. "
— JAMES MADISON (1751-1836) FOURTH PRESIDENT OF THE U.S.

that. We could all use a little more experience with that kind of personableness.

If there is a secret to living a life that matters; it is staying in love with what you are doing and with those whom you are with every day. Take time to assess your inter-relationship and your position within the group.

■■■■■■■■■■■■■■■■■■■

THE FUTURE OF AMERICA WILL BE WHAT YOU LEAVE BEHIND

America is the most successful whole society ever devised and brought to fruition by man in the history of the world. No other whole society has ever survived with so many freedoms intact for over two centuries. At any point in our odyssey, a manifold amount of our population thought the entire fabric of this country was coming unraveled. This is the reason why this unique amalgamation of people continue to co-exist.

You are important. You can make a difference. You matter. Trust in the basic goodness of every individual and derive from beliefs in our age-old teaching doctrines. The most developed and successful countries today are characterized by a high degree of trust as pointed out by Frances Fukuyama in Trust: The Social Virtues and the Creation of Prosperity. His success examples show a willingness to do business with those outside one's immediate family. Slowly developing third world countries are characterized by a high degree of distrust and skepticism. Our desire to embrace the future and new technology is based on a continuing mutual trust rooted in past experiences. We are willing to buy and invest. Trust is why our world continues to improve. We give others a chance to prove themselves. When they do, trust improves. Trust is the way to stop wars, therefore let us work with our so-called enemies. Paul Zane Pilsen, an economist, puts it differently but the effect is the same. He talks about our populations willingness to invest (trust) in ourselves (our future) by pointing to sewer systems. Eighty-five percent of America's population are on a sewer system; 57% of Europe and 37% of Japan.

We are a variety of complex patterns. The warp and woof of this country, the Black and White, the East and West, is the threaded texture that we are. What if you could get just a few more people to agree with Albert Einstein's answer to why we are here? "To serve others." Just having the right attitude can make all the difference.

" The spirit of self-help is the root of all genuine growth in the individual; and, exhibited in the lives of many, it constitutes the true source of national vigour and strength. "
— SAMUEL SMILES (1812-1904) SCOTTISH WRITER

Do We Still Have Roots in America?

You bet. They are deep and are inherent within each of us. They cannot be removed. America is as much a part of you as your family is. Deep down within us is the belief that each of us is a citizen of this great country. We have the responsibility of helping to shape the future of our community.

We must do our part to maintain a humane and responsible society in which helping hands reach out to people in honest distress. Our groups, organizations, churches and townspeople need to pull together more of us, more often, for more common needs to be met freely and fully. This is a constant educational process. Let us constantly renew our goals and remind ourselves and our children who and

" The highest patriotism and philanthropy consists, not so much in altering laws and modifying institutions, as in helping and stimulating men to elevate and improve themselves by their own free and independent individual action. "
— SAMUEL SMILES

what got us to this point. How do we do it? We do it by simply asking, by setting an example, by doing—it will happen.

Re-enforcing Our Foundations to Last

The reason America has survived for over two centuries is the process. Our founding fathers established a process we could all live under successfully. Today the whole world seems to be moving toward our mixture of individual rights and socialized government. Our constitution survives, but what of those who apply it today?

This book sets out to do something similar with familiar foundation blocks. Our goal is to carefully outline a process to reinforce those blocks, using fresh mortar to revive successful teams that can last as long as needed.

Our "Teamwork Process" is based on a long history of human ideals and values. Our collective goal is fulfilling all our human needs and aspirations. We will go through the following chapters with mortar and handy trowel. Coming chapters will review the foundation, walls and hallways you have to build, or repair, for a stronger and sturdier organization with even better leadership and understanding in place at every level. There are typical problems to be expected when any group of people join together to accomplish something. Look for answers and solutions in here.

As the process evolves for you, this book series is meant to be a ready reference and coach for facing most situations as they come up.

THE DAILY SENTINEL OBITUARY:
"Having had no children; nor relatives or friends that they were speaking to, Mr. and Mrs. Wetookitwithus decided not to leave anything to anyone. Mr. W. had said, 'If it was free it wouldn't be worth anything to anyone anyway.' So they snubbed the world and had their stuff buried with them."

Powerful Goals Overcome Apathy and Indifference

Spreading human inertia is a cancer in society especially as we live so much longer and "have seen it all". This is how a society decays. Lack of vision. One person can make a tremendous difference if that individual will dream huge dreams and start tremendous ideas rolling. Satisfying our material needs is what our politicians try to do today. Little effort and less convincing are needed because few of us can refuse the easy handout. It is the massive action that Joseph McClendon III talks about in the book Unlimited Power, A Black Choice that he co-wrote with Anthony Robbins;

"You can create changes and results most people never dream of. If you'll stop sitting around talking about it, planning it, thinking about it, and instead, actually DO IT— whatever 'it' is that can move you forward. All journeys start with the first step. Massive, committed, focused, passionate action sends a clear-cut message to the world that you are here to play to win. And the world has no choice but to sit up and take notice—and start the delivery process to hand you your desires."

#3: TAKING CHARGE OF YOUR LIFE DURING AND AFTER WORK

You are who I am talking to. I am not talking about a close friend of yours, that you admire, who you think could easily get involved in this. I would like to request that you put yourself in this picture. Quiet that little small voice in the background:

"I was meaning to ask if you thought that I might... that I could really be somebody. Me. You know what I mean? To be somebody really successful? Well, ah, waddya think?"

The answer is absolutely. You can do it. These next four chapters have the potential to change your happiness levels in easy step-by-step ways. If you will stay with me in this moment, and put real mental energy into it.

> *"For example, our most controversial value—one that was narrowly approved—speaks to our commitment to the community. It was also the one I argued most heatedly for. And today, it's one our entire organization supports fervently."*
> —MORT MEYERSON, CEO, PEROT SYSTEMS *(FAST COMPANY, 1997)*

Business is a Metaphor for Life

Fast changing businesses and the individuals within them realize more than ever that while racing into the future they must always have one foot on firm ground. That grounding has a moral and spiritual substrate within it which the workings of a free society depends.

Success, not profit, is the main focus of most prosperous companies. Success results from people helping people! Businesses grow more successful becoming really profitable, when their employees are excited about the business. They are happy at home and within the community. The most successful business makes it all achievable. Businesses rely on their communities for the talent, resources and suppliers that they need. Businesses are best served when youth, education, the environment, and the quality of life are improved.

Volunteering is natural and innate Within us

The perception that volunteering is usually hard work for no money, is rather deeply ingrained in our psyche. So, what are the benefits for you? I hear a couple of jaded souls in the back saying, "There are none!" When the drill sergeant barks for one volunteer to step forward, the platoon takes that savvy "heee-up", one step backward, leaving the newest recruit up front, volunteered.

" Knowledge is experience, anything else is just information. "
— ALBERT EINSTEIN

Consider for a moment that an excellent volunteer is a selfish volunteer not one that is selfless. Imagine that being selfish is a requirement to be a good volunteer.

A friend heard this and said, "That's not true. I'll give you an example of a really good volunteer who's not the least bit selfish, he just keeps giving and giving. He'd been happily married and he lost his job and his wife left him. He'd been going to therapy and nothing was bringing him out of his funk. He was off to himself all the time. Finally this depressed man decided he had to get out and do something for others to be with others, to get his mind off his problems. He joined Habitat for Humanity and has been constructing houses for families. He's been doing it now for years."

What a great story. And why does he continue helping after all the selfless volunteers got bored, tired, or just unappreciated, and left? Why? Why is he still doing it? He is doing it because of something deep down inside of him that needs fulfillment. He's doing it for his own reasons, he's really doing it for himself. The dictionary defines that as selfish.

The best, the very best, the most successful people in this world, are motivated by emotions deep down inside of themselves. The best songs, the best poetry and artwork come from intertwined experiences. Even countries—look how America got started. Do you think that was selflessness? Let's consider that this Country got started because of selfishness. They were concerned about themselves, selfish for their families, selfish for what it was they represented, selfish about right and wrong. And they had the stamina to see it through!

Let's look at a selfless act. Selfless people are good people, well meaning, but as you will see they have no staying power. They're in it for the image, a quick "feel good." An example is my wife, who became a brownie troop leader for selfish reasons—she wanted to have a better excuse to spend more time with her granddaughters. Here again, selfish was good. When someone takes on responsibility for twenty other girls about the

> *"Do not let yourselves be tainted by a deprecating and barren skepticism, do not let yourselves be discouraged by the sadness of certain hours which pass over nations. Live in the serene peace of laboratories and libraries. Say to yourselves first: What have I done for my instruction? and, as you gradually advance, What have I done for my country? until the time comes when you may have the immense happiness of thinking that you have contributed in some ways to the progress and good of humanity.*
> — LOUIS PASTEUR (1822-1895)FRENCH CHEMIST-MICROBIOLOGIST

same age, preparing everything to have an interesting meeting, they can get weary of it pretty darn quick unless there is some benefit in it for themselves. Selfless literally means having little or no concern for oneself. Many people admire selfless people. Do doctors think highly of patients with no concern for themselves?

The Best Part of Volunteering is How Good You Feel

The benefits of volunteering exist when it comes from the heart, from deep-down inside ourselves.

Albert Einstein was asked, "What is the meaning of life?" He answered without hesitation, "Service to others." Is this the secret of a happy life? Service to others? How will we reconcile selfishness and service to others? Well, isn't that also a good definition of a successful business person? Someone with a deep down internal drive, either sees a service or need that could be satisfied at a profit, or produces something that people want and will pay to acquire.

So, how do we turn all volunteers into deeply concerned, sensitive, caring volunteers? The best place to start is by making sure everyone understands the ground rules. It starts with who you are to everyone else. This concerns your integrity and your character, solid grounding in the basics that all the great books teach.

If you are concerned and very selfish about protecting your basic needs and you selfishly share that with others, you can achieve success. It is necessary to share with others to become successful. The results are exciting and infectious. Others see the fire of your desire to be a winner. By helping you, they see how they will be winners too. In turn you will want to help them to be winning volunteers.

Business has a responsibility to be a good citizen. We see that business people who accept the responsibility of stewardship, goodwill and fairness in their community find that, "Somehow...it always pays off."

"Life is not easy for any of us. But what of that? We must have perseverance and above all confidence in ourselves. We must believe that we are gifted for something, and that this thing, at whatever cost, must be attained."
— MARIE CURIE (1867-1934)
POLISH CHEMIST

#4. HOW ABOUT YOUR HAPPINESS?

■■■■■■■■■■■■■■■■■■■■■

The world's most successful business people have very successful family lives. They are some of the longest lived and hardest working individuals. They have a highly effective support system. They are loved—and they love. They are aware of the most important things in life. The most love you can feel is the love you radiate. Action—reaction.

Peter Drucker, a well known business development and management expert, has written a book on non-profits in which he says:

> "Developing yourself begins by serving, by striving toward an idea outside of yourself—not by leading. Leaders are not born, nor are they made—they are self-made. To do this, a person needs focus. I do it by asking people what they want to be remembered for. According to St. Augustine, "that's the beginning of adulthood."

It's possible for anyone to do something wonderful in their life, they just have to decide to do it.

In Pursuit of Your Self-Esteem

What do you expect the inner personal feelings of people at the top of the ladder would be? Why not jot down the answers that just flew through the thought passages of your mind. Perhaps you have thought that pride was most important? And money was not at all important? You would be right. These people have all the money they want. People with great pride are easily recognized, they are greatly appreciated and they are loved. Opportunity and money seem to just flow to them. Pride is not something you just assume one day, or get by doing heroic work. You gain it over time. Self esteem is an internal opinion of yourself based on feedback from others. The more self respect you give to others, the more you feel within yourself. It is your deep-down interests that propel you to accomplish great things.

Sisyphus was a forced volunteer (a fallen king) shown here at his after-work recreation. After all is said and done will it have been only your job and family that mattered? Or, will your life be fuller than that?

How often is it that any of us make a clear choice about our future and achieve it? Certainly by the fourth grade, most of us have self-judged that we are about "so bright". A lot of our friends, peers, or neighbors we know: our parents and friends of theirs, are all doing a type of thing called "work." The pay is okay, "So, I'll do something like that!" Even worse, we go into clubs, organizations and volunteering with the same attitude. Luckily we are an adaptable people and have the ability to "fit" in most situations.

The benefits of volunteering can only be realized when each of us takes charge of our own lives. When we do, we know that being an mediocre volunteer is not "okay". You have already had enough "experience" with "okay" environments. You are able to make your own choices in at least what you are volunteering to do!

What is your usual life like? Are you totally absorbed in your own world? Volunteer organizations get people to open up, to see, and work with a wider variety of other outreaching individuals.

It is possible for anyone to do something wonderful in their life, they just have to decide to do it.

Absolutely critical to the success of your community is your personal happiness. Let's be really selfish about you. If you can realize and appreciate how satisfied and successful you can be, the value and success of the rest of your life is assured.

Practice being excited, happy, satisfied and excellent in what you do after work,

"The man who regards his own life and that of his fellow creatures as meaningless is not merely unfortunate but almost disqualified for life."
— ALBERT EINSTEIN (1879-1955) SWISS-AMERICAN PHYSICIST

"We can't do everything at once, but we can do something at once."
—CALVIN COOLIDGE (1872-1933) 30TH PRESIDENT OF THE U.S.

"One can never consent to creep when one feels an impulse to soar."
—HELEN KELLER (1880-1968) U.S. LECTURER, AUTHOR, AND EDUCATOR

and the results will be soon apparent in the "work place" of your life as well. All this "new you", of your own choosing, will soon enough be reflected in your new character.

What Constitutes the Good Life?

"Americans are already the most generous people on earth, contributing more than $120 billion per year to organized private charity."
— Michael Tanner 1996

"Donations to charity rise 7.5%. Americans gave $143.5-billion in '97; international causes did best."
—The Chronicle of Philanthropy, 1998

The 1998 findings of the National Survey on Philanthropy and Civic Renewal disputes most media findings that Americans are generally selfish. Individuals have given $110 billion to charity which is 10 times the amount of giving by all the foundations in the United States combined. Corporations and bequests average about 20 billion.

Another survey notes that Baby Boomers believe they have more than their parents; better cars, better homes, more of the material things. Does this bring happiness? No. Boomers also said in the survey that their parents were generally happier than they themselves are.

What happened? Well, it's our changing cause and effect. According to William J. Bennett, births out of wedlock have gone from 5 percent in 1960 to 31 percent in 1992. Divorce has quadrupled in that time. Violent crime is up 560 percent. Scholastic aptitude is down. Teen delinquency and suicide are up. Why? Why? Why?

Our actions have caused these reactions to build up over the past 40 years. We set out as a nation to satisfy the needs of our country through The Great Society. We seriously thought we could pay others to dole out the food and the money. We stopped having to feel and care personally. We are all much less happy as a result.

It appears we have not stayed focused on what has worked so well. As Earl Nightingale in Lead the Field said:

> "If a great discovery was made in a particular generation you might think all the succeeding generations would know about it and utilize it. But in many areas this is not the case.
>
> While true of most inventions and discoveries it frequently is not true when it comes to the great laws that determine the direction of our individual destinies.
>
> One such great law on which everything in the universe operates is the law of cause and effect. This law has been written thousands of times by the greatest minds the world has produced and as a result, it has appeared in many forms.
>
> For our purposes it may be best to put it this way: Our rewards in life will always match our service. It's another way of saying, "As you sow, so shall ye reap."

"As Ye Sow, So Shall Ye Reap."

Let's spend a minute here and ponder this great law, "As ye sow, so shall ye reap." How can the amount we put into something always return? Rather unbelievable on the surface isn't it? Does this mean if you give a twenty dollar bill to a homeless drunk that you will get it back later somehow? The answer, of course, is yes. Allow me to explain.

"Man is more fundamentally a co-operative animal than a competitive animal. His survival as a species has been perhaps through mutual aid rather than through rugged individualism. And somehow it has been ground into us by the forces of evolution to be 'instinctively' happiest over those things which in the long run yield the greatest good to the greatest number.
— BILHSJSLMUT
DYRGSNDDON
(1879-1962)
ANTHROPOLOGIST

You can sow negatively as easily as positively. How you choose to sow is as important as the actual sowing. Someone might think they are helping a homeless drunk by giving him twenty dollars. In actuality, they may be hurting him by encouraging him to his demise of eventually being found face down in the gutter. The giver's reward for giving twenty dollars worth of hard-earned money to a homeless drunk may further the blight in the community.

If we choose to sow by giving twenty dollars worth of our precious time in helping this man sober up, clean up, and get to an Alcoholics Anonymous meeting, we may reap rewards far greater. This same man may even mend his ways and go on to help others.

But what if a giver chooses to "sow" by giving his twenty dollars to a nearby church, pointing out that his money is to help that drunk over there? This choice is a less personally responsible road. The rewards may or may not be as great. Certainly doing the helping yourself offers up additional personal rewards from the experience by actually doing the helping. You may learn a lot more about yourself in the process.

The ease or difficulty of your efforts may encourage other ideas which could salvage even more lives by reworking the standard road back to productive citizenry easier to accomplish somehow.

Finally, our giver could simply vote for a tax and let the local government handle it. This least personally responsible method is certainly the easiest. It shows that this person is at least conscious of the need and is willing to do something. Maybe you presume that what you "sow" in this manner is a positive and that you should reap only positive. Not so. If you thoughtlessly choose to cast your seeds on the rocks, that is "as ye sow" and even with adequate water and sun "so ye shall reap" will still be an inferior result. Contributing to a program that coninues shabby treatment of this man and he may be around to assault you the next time? That then is your repayment.

The focus here is being selfish for you. You are the most important planter of all. If you aren't in the right frame of mind, how can you be expected to do the right thing? People who simply give without working out the why, can't fully appreciate the rewards which come from intelligent giving. They put out a half-baked gift and receive the same in return. It cheapens the whole experience for everyone involved, they feel under-appreciated. What a shame. This giving person usually "burns out" in a very short time.

Sowing and reaping is the action and reaction we've talked about. The positive or negative we put in is proportional to the positive or negative we get out. Whether or not we are completely conscious of it.

How Businesses Help Their Communities by Not Writing a Check to Charity!

Rather than contributing corporate money directly to charities, many prominent businesses are encouraging their employees to contribute more and more time to a cause they believe in.

Research today continues to cite stress as a cause for cancer. Interestingly, couch potato types suffer a lot of stress. Mainly from frustration, lack of focus, and no accomplishment. Even the smallest of goals evolves into a sense of balance and liberation. Hard work, even overwork, does not cause stress. Stress is how we mentally feel about it. For example, instead of writing a check to charity, one very large business has an office that aids their employees in carrying out their own contributions to the community. For example, helping at a senior center or an orphanage, or teaching English as-a-second-language at a local school.

More and more businesses realize that personal problems at home and in the community are potential opportunities to expand employee potential. These problems have a direct impact on the work environment.

"Know thyself."

—PLATO

"This above all, to thine own self be true."

SHAKESPEARE, "HAMLET"

"A man is least known to himself."

—CICERO, FROM "DE ORATORE"

"Every new adjustment is a crisis in self-esteem."

—ERIC HOFFER IN "THE ORDEAL OF CHANGE"

"Resolve to be thyself; and know that he who finds himself, loses his misery!"

—MATTHEW ARNOLD, FROM "SELF DEPENDENCE"

"Self love my liege, is not so vile a sin as self-neglecting."

SHAKESPEARE, "HENRY V"

"Self-contempt, bitterer to drink than blood"

—SHELLEY, FROM "PROMETHEUS UNBOUND"

#5: ANALYZING YOURSELF, YOUR DIRECTION AND GOALS

■■■■■■■■■■■■■■■■■■

What is Your Definition of "The Good Life?"

Time after time the answer comes back; "I want to be with people I love, in a place that gives me the sense of belonging, doing purposeful work that fits what I do best."

Isn't this the number one thing every one of us must eventually come to grips with to be happy? Absolutely critical to the success of your community is your happiness. Let's be really selfish about you. If you can appreciate and realize how satisfied and successful you can be, the value and success for the rest of your life is assured.

Practice being exciting, happy, satisfied and excellent in what you do. This new you of your own choosing will soon be reflected in your new character.

"We can't do everything at once, but we can do something at once."
—Calvin Coolidge

"Beyond a certain point in one's career, cash is not all that important. One returns again to the value of the experience offered by the job, the challenge to test one's own mettle, and also the fun, the enjoyment, the pride, and the sense of self-fulfillment that hard work can offer"
—HAROLD GENEEN, CEO, ITT. 1964—1984

Having the whole knowledge picture is most important for selfish satisfaction and for a satisfactory world. You and I are here on earth to make the most of ourselves. The most we can do is to pay close attention passing that information along to the next generation. We must always be in service to others to be fulfilled.

Oliver Wendall Holmes ends one of this poems this way, "Most people go to their graves with their music still in them". If you only had six months to live what would you do...six weeks, six days, six hours, or six minutes? Write your own obituary. What you think most, you will become. Separate worries outside your realm and confront what you can have an impact upon. Work with what you can change. Honesty and integrity cannot be rushed. They are the most rewarding ways to get rich.

Most Americans are already the richest people on earth. We have the greatest choices as to how we spend our time. Whatever we do, let's give it our best. Let's have an open mind to other ideas. We are only going to receive in return what we put in. This is because we know deep inside how well we did our job. This same all-knowing inner eye also senses how those around us are doing. Are we keeping up with them or are they keeping up with our interest and our vigor. Our drive for knowledge and continuing improvement? Wherever we find an interesting person like this, we have found a leader, a most valuable person. I believe you are that person—at whatever level you are comfortable with. You are a thinker, you offer solutions not problems. You are a sponge for information tools that help you gain knowledge moving you toward your goal. You are happy with a deep-down satisfaction that comes from doing the worthwhile things your heart desires. You are not impatient. You have faith that what should come to you, will come to you.

You know that success, like honesty and integrity, does not come naturally. Our inborn instinct is survival and that is to take, take, take for ourselves. Working as part of a team and sharing our experiences creates the synergy that prduces mankind's greatest achievements. You know that it is service to others that brings the greatest personal satisfactions. Whatever you shall sow you shall reap. We have our free will and a certain amount of time to use it.

Your Own Snapshot of Your life

Taking time to analyze yourself is the most incredible gift you can give yourself and to those around you. Please make a special time to sit down and leisurely comprehend "you" as you go through this chapter.

Let's start by asking, "How open-minded are you?" "Very," is the expected reply. "I am right! If I was wrong I would, of course, change my mind. So, you see, I am open minded." Certainly. It's all those other people that have the closed minds.

When we have lived a long time with a negative attitude, behavior, or belief, it is difficult to see and own up to a changed reality. Examples of past mental blocks may still be race and gender equality. Some of us continue to burden ourselves with anger or angst over the mere mention of these should-be-dead issues. What huge strides we will make when we can all let go of our prejudices.

When we are looking inwardly and planning for the future, we must first admit that we are our own biggest impediment to success. We must be open to new ideas which may be foreign to us, but are usually age old. What seems to be the obvious solutions to maladies such as crime, welfare, and education, are not solutions at all. As Thoreau said: "For every thousand hacking at the leaves of evil, there is one striking at the root."

When we create our own problems, or allow life to happen to us, through half-heartedness or thoughtlessness, we cannot change at that level of focus. Friends can tell us, but we ourselves can't see it. We must view it, usually much later, at a different level of thinking, from an alternative perspective. Hopefully this is that moment for you. Have a pen and paper handy to outline your goals. You will want to save these in a notebook to look back at later.

Let's Paint a Picture of You

To break out of our thickly-encrusted self-chrome-plating of personal identity and protectiveness, let's look at ourselves in a totally new way. Yes, let's look at our life as likened to a bucket of paint.

Every life is full, whether a person lives days or decades. Each is a full life. This can of paint is always full. What color is your can of paint? On one end of the color spectrum, we have white which is ascribed to purity, saintliness, and the goals we are supposed to strive for. On the other end is black—the dark side. What color are you today? Do you wear "a coat of many colors"? Oddly enough, a coat of many colors may become white. If you paint the blades of a fan in true primary and true secondary colors equally, then turn it on, what one color would you be looking at? White. Black is the absence of all color. The same goes for us. We are all a variety of colors. If you radiate the fullness of a colorful life and have balance throughout you are probably a saint. If you are transparent, dull, drab, muddy, tasteless, mediocre—you are well into the other end of the spectrum.

Now, mentally lift the lid from your can of paint. Inside, we see a picture painted of you. Start in close on your face. What is the expression on your face at this moment? Are you busy or relaxed? Are you posing for this picture? Is it a sharp, clear picture, or is the paint a bit mixed with soft edges? Slowly pull back to view the full scene. Describe the picture you see in a couple of sentences. Be honest about your feelings, don't color them brighter than they are. This is for your eyes only. Use this device to think of yourself in a very different way—from the mirror in. Your mind is already accomplishing this as you are reading—stop now and jot down your thoughts. What colors do you see? Are there splotches or swirls of color? Chock-a-block? Mostly one color with a sprinkling or big doses of this and that color? Is it a portrait? Are you alone in this picture?

This is who you are. Not what you want others to think you are. When you contemplate what you want, examine what you are good at too. Take a moment to write down quickly what you see now. Don't over think your feelings just now. Just get it out on paper.

On a scale of one-to-ten, how satisfied are you now with this picture? Ten being the most satisfied.

*Look at
yourself in
a different
way...*

When you are finished, consider what you wish the picture looked like. Flavor your Garden of Colors. Your life cannot be equally all colors of the rainbow. Indeed, the rainbow is finally perceived as only the three primary colors. Is your future subdued and stately with well-positioned flairs of color? Is it to be bright and sunshiny? Darker colors and browns are conservative.

Write down your current colors and the future colors you would rather be. Now, on a scale of one to ten how overall happy will you be wearing this color mantel? Write down a date when you want to be in this new picture or desire to be in it.

If Money Was of No Concern, What Would you Change?

Write what you would stop doing if money were no longer a concern for you. Think also of all the trivial things you would probably stop doing. Now, list what you would start doing. Stretch to think of trivial little things you would take time to do or have. What would your worldly possessions look like: car, house, animals, clothes, hobbies, collections?

In imagining your new life, write down where your ongoing satisfaction comes from. Not the easy smiles, but the deep-down long-term-satisfaction smiles. What will you be smiling about in your mind as you lie on your deathbed looking back over your life? Did you choose the right things to do? Were you always chasing the almighty dollar? How effective will you have been?

"The body of Benjamin Franklin, Printer (like the cover of an old book, its contents torn out and stripped of its lettering and gilding), lies here, food for worms; but the work shall not be lost, for it will (as he believed) appear once more in a new and more elegant edition, revised and corrected by the Author."

—Benjamin Franklin (1706-1790) (epitaph composed for himself in 1728)

Benjamin Franklin believed in reincarnation. Is that you? Are you Benjamin Franklin in a new skin? Yes, he could be you! It's been said that man becomes what he thinks about all the time. Do you think Ben Franklin thoughts?

#6: HOW EXCITING, COLORFUL AND MOTIVATED ARE YOU?

This is your test, you decide

**Is your life lots of little busy-ness, chores not all that satisfying?
Or is your life energy put to fewer more significant goals?
Think of things you do, then roughly scribble or paint the amount
of weekly time spent visually into your picture.
The lighter brighter colors are what you enjoy most.
The numbers represent how much time
you spend doing these things.**

Big   Also   Moving   Tops
Zero   Ran   Up   100%

Look back into your gallon of paint one more time. Imagine each of your future life satisfaction items as a color taking up a portion of the space in the can. Their importance and the time involved are equally proportionate to, and relative to, the other colors in the gallon paint can of your whole life. You may choose to think of it as a pie chart. Hold a mental snapshot of what you see, like memorizing a phone number. Pick out no more than seven colors that dominate. Hold them lightly in your mind. Write down the size dollops of each color quadrants within the big circle. Give each color a percentage, so when they all add up they are 100 percent of the picture. Be descriptive of your colors.

Make a pie chart (paint can lid?) or simply assign percentages to each item that ultimately total around one hundred percent.

You now have an indication of how much time you must spend toward the goals you have expressed for yourself in this chart versus the colors in the original drawing. All the potential that you see in there is up to you.

Now let's benchmark the extremes of your color chart to see where you have put yourself. Imagine someone who is the epitome, right now, of where you want to be. This person does not have to be famous nor do you have to know him or her very well. Your mental perception is all that counts here. Take a snapshot of his/her face, the expression, the pose or action. Slowly pull back and describe the scene—who they are with and the five to seven major colors that surround the person. Sketch this out with quick notes about what you are seeing. Use circles or pie wedge quadrants to indicate major areas of interest that make up this person. Is work 65 percent of this person's life, 15 percent outside activity, 10 percent family, and 2 percent religion?

Now go to the opposite side. Who do you really dislike? Who is the most reprehensible, or really sad person you can think of? Sketch circles and color, indicating percentages of this person. Now on this, the fairest scale of all—which is completely your creation, mentally place the bad guy at zero on one end and your "goal guy" at 100 percent on the other. Where do you place yourself along this line? No excuses. Don't blame heredity, or others—it's up to you.

The most powerful application of this exercise is to carry a colorful picture of your hero/mentor in your mind. Yes, also in your wallet, and on the wall. This can be a photo from a magazine to which you add colors. What is best is your own very colorful rendering. Even if it is merely a stick figure done with crayons, it's the colors you want to move toward. It is the image that you are striving toward. Keep this physical reminder. Your sub-conscious will fill in for your lack of drawing ability and move in that direction.

Another application of this is to search for a painting that has the colors you are moving toward. The subject can be anything—it's the colors that are inspiring you; constantly reminding you. Only you will know how powerful that picture is to you. How uplifting and inspiring it is to you. You will become those colors in no time at all, feel, think, and express them. Why? Because your mind has little learned baggage encumbering it and telling you how you cannot achieve this.

Our emotions rule us. No amount of facts and information will get us out of bed. We must be stimulated by our own desire. What keeps us from becoming a puddle of drool, strapped into a wheelchair?

Our desire to "matter" is what gets us up from our catatonic state every morning. As we come up out of our rem sleep into the bright light of morning, we ascend like a bird up into

" This is the true joy of life, the being used for a purpose recognized by yourself as a mighty one; the being a force of nature instead of a feverish selfish little clod of ailments and grievances complaining that the world will not devote itself to making you happy. I want to be thoroughly used up when I die, for the harder I work the more I live. I rejoice in life for its own sake. Life is no "brief candle" to me. It is a sort of splendid torch which I have got hold of for the moment, and I want to make it burn as brightly as possible before handing it on to future generations. "
— GEORGE BERNARD SHAW

the heavenly day to whatever level we self-choose. Let's self-choose something better for you.

Let's go for deep-down satisfaction and pride. It will take a ton of daily work in some peoples' minds—not yours.

■■■■■■■■■■■■■■■■■■■

BECOMING THE "YOU"-YOU'D LOVE

Living Longer Has More to do With Your State of Mind

"I don't know what your destiny will be, but one thing I do know: The only ones among you who will be really happy are those who will have sought and found how to serve."
— ALBERT SCHWEITZER
(1875-1965)
ALSATIAN-BORN MEDICAL
MISSIONARY

Hard mental and physical work doesn't kill people. It is anger, worry, depression, and feelings of uselessness, which send us to an early grave. Think of leaders in large organizations and countries who live well into their eighties and nineties. Norman Vincent Peale affirms this:

Dr. Flanders Dunbar, author of Mind and Body says; "It is not a question of whether an illness is physical or emotional, but how much of each. Every thoughtful person who has ever considered the matter realizes that the doctors are right when they tell us that resentment, hate, grudge, ill will, jealousy, vindictiveness, are attitudes which produce ill health. Have a fit of anger and experience for yourself that sinking feeling in the pit of your stomach, that sense of stomach sickness. Chemical reactions in the body are set up by emotional outbursts that result in feelings of ill-health. Should these be continued either violently or in a simmering state over a period of time, the general condition of the body will deteriorate.

So if you are under par I suggest that you do a

very scrupulous job of self-analysis. Honestly ask yourself if you are harboring any ill will or resentment or grudges, and if so cast them out. Get rid of them without delay. They do not hurt anybody else, but every day and every night of your life they are eating at you. Many people suffer poor health not because of what they eat, but from what is eating them. Emotional ills turn in upon yourself, sapping your energy, reducing your efficiency, causing deterioration in our health. And of course they siphon off your happiness."

Shall we reverse the typical learning curve in our life?

Long term leadership requires knowledge and understanding. Not only of the jobs to be done by the people you work with, but about people in general. To know people is to really understand yourself better.

The Japanese believe the older you are the more you need to study. Can this be why we have so many wise old sayings from Japanese history? Do young people there still seek out and cherish their elders for advice? Can this be why they are still so revered and cared for and live longer?

The Power of Positive Thinking

Hundreds of books and articles were researched to do this book series. If there was one book I would ask you to absorb it is The Power of Positive Thinking by Norman Vincent Peale. No matter that this is a decades old book. No other single recommendation will do more to free your mind to be fully successful. Peale is a master motivator and storyteller. Here he talks with probably World War II's most famous pilot:

" Success is the progressive realization of a worthy goal or the pursuit of a worthy ideal. "

—ANONYMOUS

"I have always been an admirer of Eddie

Rickenbacker and I commented on his lack of tension. 'I know how busy you are,' I said, 'and I marvel at the way you sit quiet, composed, and peaceful like. Eddie, I know you have some technique to attain this impressive serenity. Tell me about it, please.'

He gave me a formula which he says he uses frequently. Now I use it myself and it is very effective:

First, collapse physically. Practice this several times a day. Let go every muscle in the body. Conceive of yourself as a jellyfish, getting your body into complete looseness. Form a mental picture of a huge burlap bag of potatoes. Then mentally cut the bag, allowing the potatoes to roll out. Think of yourself as the bag.

What is more relaxed than an empty burlap bag?

The second element is to 'drain the mind' of all irritation, all resentment, all frustration, several times a day.

Third, think spiritually, which means to turn the mind at regular intervals to God. At least three times a day 'lift up your eyes unto the hills.' This keeps you in tune with God's harmony. It refills you with peace."

Peale urges us to be everything we can be, to hold nothing back. He says:

"A famous trapeze artist was instructing his students how to perform on the high trapeze bar. Finally, having given full explanations and instruction in this skill, he told them to demonstrate their ability. One student, looking up at the insecure perch upon which he must perform, was suddenly filled with fear. The instructor put his arm around the boy's shoulder and said, 'Son, you can do it, and I will tell you how.' Then he made a statement which is of inestimable importance. He said, 'Throw your heart over the bar and you body will follow.'

Copy that one sentence. Write it on a card and put in your pocket. Place it under the glass on your desk top. Tack it up on your wall. Stick it on your (bathroom) mirror. Better still,write it on your mind, you who really want to do something with life. It's packed with power, that sentence."

Are you willing to make a commitment to change or action and put your whole heart into it?

Failing is Practice for Success

- Dr. Theodore Geisel Seuss' first childrens book was rejected by twenty-three publishers. The twenty-fourth sold six million copies.

- Babe Ruth struck out 1,330 times while amassing 714 home runs.

- Abraham Lincoln failed twice in business and was defeated six times in state and national elections before being elected President of the United States.

Never worry about failure. It is failure that breeds the intense desire for success. No one is born doing things even well. We start out stumbling and falling until we get it right. The same thing happens through school, on the job and certainly within organizations. Allow others to experiment and fail too. The death of an organization comes when experimenting dies.

Keep the interest alive. Satisfaction and pride comes from a job well done. Not the same old job done the same old way. Take on risk yourself. Don't be afraid to experiment. Honor your risk takers, acknowledge their undertaking and the results. Reward yourself, and others, for good attempts too. When you decide on a course, stick with it through the difficult times that inevitably come. Keep faith in what you do and have patience—you will succeed.

> *"Education is a social process. Education is growth. Education is not preparation for life; education is life itself."*
> —JOHN DEWEY (1859-1952) U.S. PHILOSOPHER AND EDUCATOR

> *"Failure in any good cause is honorable... it is not the result that is to be regarded so much as the aim and the effort, the patience, the courage, and the endeavour with which desirable and worthy objects are pursued."*
> — SAMUEL SMILES (1812-1904) SCOTTISH WRITER

#7. HOW PEOPLE-WEALTHY ARE YOU?

■■■■■■■■■■■■■■■■■■■■■■

In order to put your life-to-date in perspective, let's imagine you as a potential stock market investment. How people invested are you now? In time of trouble, how many would come to your aid? Is this a true benefit of volunteering?

Many people when they get thoroughly bored, depressed or otherwise off their map of things that they do daily, don't take time to realize how valuable they are. Not in a monetary way but in a social relationship way. When we have an identity crisis, for instance, when we lose our job, or start muddling over the mid-life routine we're tired of, or the same old cul-de-sac we are in. We need to stop and take stock of ourselves. When someone new asks about you, what do you say you are as a person? Your Job? "I'm a computer operator," or, "I'm a truck driver." Let's take a look at the whole you.

Deep Down Satisfaction Starts Right Here With Your Personal Relationships

"How ya' doin'?"

On a blank piece of paper, writing somewhat small, put your name in the center of it. Circle it. Above your name draw a vertical line. Enclose yourself with an outer circle. Going clockwise spoke out similar lines at 3:00, 6:00, and 9:00 o'clock. Within these four quadrants add names to what you will regard as your investment or personal network. Include the names clockwise according to your personal and emotional closeness and importance to you. Your spouse would be at 12:01, very important and near your name. Very important but not close (your boss might be an example)—put those types out near the fringes of the paper. Balance your opposite end of 11:00 o'clock with someone distant in time or miles but still a contact. An old high school buddy may fit. Is that school friend just a contact or someone you

Your People Investment Pie Chart

The innermost circle are those you feel closest to. The very closest of those are in the noon to three o'clock quadrant.

Adding arrows show the direction those relationships are headed, or a direction you want them to go with added attention.

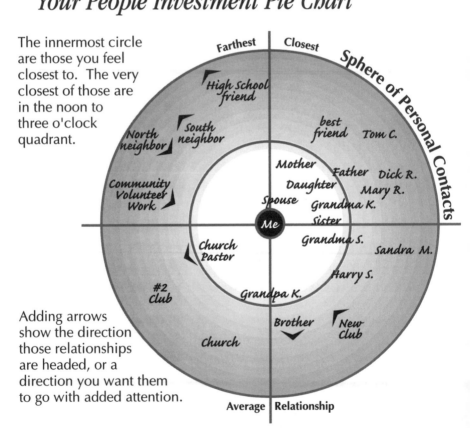

---

haven't talked to for years and yet could confide something personal. If personal, put him or her closer in at 11:00 o'clock. If just a contact, move the name out to the fringes. Quickly add names as they occur to you. Neighbors would be listed, though possibly out on the fringes at 11:00 o'clock. Casual friends who come for dinner will probably be in your 3:00 to 6:00 quadrant. Friends in your volunteer group may be spread from 3:00 to 11:00 o'clock.

Draw a loose inner circle, with your name as the center, that encompasses most of your 'close' contacts. You are now looking at a snapshot of the people in your life today and their relative importance to you. This should take only five or ten minutes. You may want to date this sheet and save it as a mile marker to refer back to at a future date.

Let's take our People Investment Pie Chart and make it work a little harder. Note with an arrow which person is moving into your life or away from you. No arrow means they are stable with you. With another colored pen, note the direction you would like certain people to move with you. Some of these names you may want to put on your "TO DO" list or on your short term or long term goal list. This sheet could create some tremendous satisfaction for you later on.

Let's work up some personal contact assumptions together:

• **If you have 30 or more names on the paper** and they are somewhat balanced inside and outside your personal circle—you have invested very well already. You are a rising star wherever you go in your existing local area.

Will you grow? Will you help them grow? How? By adding or changing who is distant or close? Why? There is no right or wrong, this is your universe and you should be proud with plans to continually improve your "life/friends/universe."

•**From 15 to 29** you are in a moderately good position in your overall well-being. Look where you may be losing your balance inside or outside your friendly circle of close, casual, important friends or contacts. Consider your inner circle of friends versus the external circle. Your introvertedness versus your ability to open up to outside opportunities and friends. When just looking at your close-in friends, are they clustered tightly in your first one to three quadrant? Rounding out your life takes on new meaning when you look at your snapshot of friends and associates.

•**If you have less than 15** names on this list, your network probably needs improvement. Friends, even business friends, or volunteer friends, are like an insurance policy. When you have a problem, these are the people to turn to. You need to consider how you can improve your investment in life. What you present and give out to others will come back to you in so many positive ways. Put out a little, you can expect only a little back.

You may be working too hard for the almighty dollar and not taking the necessary time-outs for family, community, and leisure. Are you trapped on the treadmill-of-work and buying what you think is happiness? The best benefit of getting to know a larger and wider array of friends is that you expand too. More opportunities open up for you. You become wealthier in every way. If you truly are currently in the best of life's investment positions, you would still want to reassure yourself and re-invigorate others. Winners want to renew and re-push the winning buttons.

Appreciate and Plan Your Life

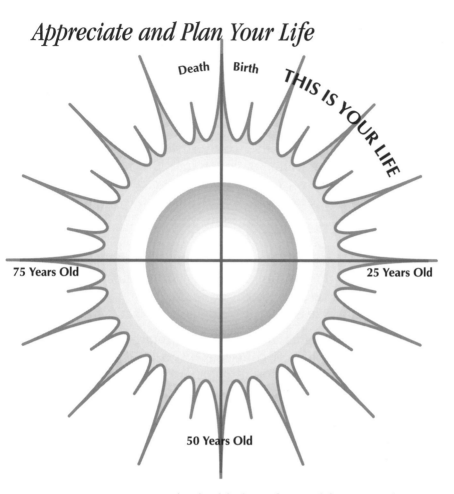

Let us appreciate the highlights of your life up until now and go on to plan your future highlights. Pencil or otherwise copy the sunburst onto a blank sheet of paper. Starting with "birth" at the top clockwise put the decades of your life assuming we will all live to 100. Tick off the point in life where you are today. On each ray of sunshine put a word or two that describes a highlight in your life starting from your first childhood memories. List what first comes to mind. Continue listing right on into your future as far as you've ever contemplated. Now go back and think a little harder about the smaller events that have colored your life. Add these to the shorter rays. If a major event occurs to you later, don't rejuggle your earlier thoughts, just add a ray where appropriate. On the future side of your sun add in the smaller, shorter goals. These are important mile markers to accomplish to realize the longer, brighter, more significant goals. If this future side is a bit of a struggle take a little time to analyze the high points you've listed. Why were they so important. Were you the initiator in every case? Or were you part of a group effort? What other patterns show up? Your past is an excellent indication of your future. Does that make you happy? Maybe with a few course corrections your smile would be bigger? What would those course corrections be? List them out. Note them on your sun rays where appropriate.

Now let's write out the speech your best friend will give at your "Lifetime Goal Achievement" award ceremony. Keep it short, no more than two or three paragraphs. Please stop reading and do that now.

The highlights noted on the future part of your sunburst rays are, of course, your goals. The "speech" is your personal mission statement. I hope you are as excited as I am about this accomplishment of yours. You are now a part of the one-half-of-one-percent of the population that even thinks about this. Statistically you are guaranteed to be more successful.

#8: WHAT IS, "LIVING A SUCCESSFUL LIFE?"

If you plan your future and work your plan; the brass ring will easily come around to you and all the success it represents to you. If you jump for it like trying to win the lottery, you are doomed to failure whether you win it or not.

Making yourself happy is most important. If you aren't happy, nobody wants to be around you. This is so important and should be obvious. Don't make yourself a martyr for others. Ask yourself, "Will this future I am moving toward be more fun than fun?" More fun than fun is deep down satisfaction! Fun is a deep-down glow which actually physically warms and tingles you when you completely stop and think about the whole of it. Your mind actually smiles about it. Satisfaction is always a result of your full and honest commitment.

In his book, <u>In Pursuit of Happiness and Good Government,</u> Charles Murray discusses happiness and pleasure:

> "For those who put their signatures to the Declaration, a society in which people were able to pursue happiness was no more and no less than a society in which people were able to go about the business of being human beings as wisely and fully as they could. The job of government was to enable them to do so. People can have no higher calling, nor can governments.
>
> Aristotle clarifies the nature of pleasure and, as might be expected, he emphatically rejects an identity of pleasure and happiness: 'That happiness is pleasurable does not mean that pleasures constitute happiness. But the happy man enjoys himself, and the happier he is, the more he enjoys himself.'"

Four More Sincere Benefits of Volunteering

"Why Volunteer? I Have to Make a Living First!" Why? For one, you will make all the money you want or need doing this! Most important, you will be happier. Being happier is the very reason money and personal success will come easier for you.

There are many other reasons. Some are logical and are reason enough by themselves. Some are intangible, but will help put you at the top of your profession. Here are four:

• **Becoming inspired.** Many other business management or leadership books discuss motivational carrots in the bundle of incentives that we can't use when we discuss the all-volunteer organization. For instance, the almighty dollar is a carrot we can very rarely use. When we can, the amount is usually an insult to the energy and quality of work the person gives us. This workbook will give you solid tools to get people motivated, to volunteer, to do very dull and mundane things like stuffing envelopes. If you and I can do that in a volunteer organization, imagine what that could mean in your business, your family—in all other aspects of your life?

"Opportunity has hair in front, behind she is bald; if you seize her by the forelock you may hold her, but, if suffered to escape, not Jupiter himself can catch her again."
— FROM THE LATIN

•**Building personal relationships.** Changing the world community begins one person at a time starting right here at home. It is a collective inspiration and focus, like a white hot light, on what works. Reviewing, mentally exercising people, and team building relationships will have direct application in your life. The tools are here to vary your approach. You will decide the paths to take.

•**Your life success** comes from exercising your thinking. Every time you think something the same way, you get a result you like, or like reasonably well enough to keep doing it. It becomes part of your routine, good and bad habits. If you keep doing things the way you've always done them, you'll get the results you've always gotten. This is how years go by in a flash. When you volunteer you are in a new environment with new approaches, new ways of doing things. A problem with many of our organizations today is that they have long ago ceased to be effective. They have ceased to be outward reaching. When you apply these ideas successfully you change as well, your people skills are sharpened, and you acquire different perspectives. Ideas in this environment, are used everywhere you go with everyone you meet. You are a more valuable person and so you will be repaid for your efforts. This book series concerns change. Are you open to change? The way to effect change in others is to begin by changes within one self.

• **Your Attitude.** Volunteer organizations force us to relate to others not as "employees or bosses," but as "associates or team members." Your attitude is the key to success. When you act as a facilitator, coordinator, or leader, rather than as a boss, people feel like they are part of your team. This is how exciting things really begin to happen. Volunteering lets us focus on the good and the positive. People will notice a difference about you. Your attitude is something people can actually see in you, hear in your voice. You will see them differently. Your job won't be your only life. Your business associates will enjoy your wider horizons.

What One Word Describes Your Drive?

To be enormously _____ (what one word will you put there?), I must work at it a little bit every day.

Earl Nightingale said,

> "People who refuse to do more than they're being paid for will seldom be paid for more than they're doing. You may have heard someone say, 'Why should I knock myself out for the money I'm getting?' It's this attitude that, more than anything else, keeps people at the bottom of the economic pile."

Focusing on Number One

How You Will Become Wealthy!

There is one extremely effective remedy to challenges of time and money. I read about it first in Napoleon Hill's legendary work Think and Grow Rich. I tried the following idea sporadically with some success and the habit fell away. The next time I heard it on a tape by Brian Tracy, he said, in effect, if you would do only two things you would make it to the top of your profession. What are the secrets of so many successful leaders? What is the one common denominator of millionaires in the making?

Charles Schwab, the man most credited with consolidating the steel industry in America, paid an efficiency expert, Ivy Lee, $25,000 for this same basic idea back when $25,000 was really a lot of money. If I reveal this very simple idea, which is also as easy to actually do as what you've been doing all your life, will you promise to do it? Are you committed at this point in your life to improving yourself and the lives of those you touch? Will you tell your spouse or close friend that you are committed to this? If you will...say so! Right out loud, right now!

There are actually three things to do that will change your life and that of the community around you, given that this is a goal of yours. But Mr. Lee's idea is the crux of it.

*" Nothing in the world can take the place of persistence. Talent will not; nothing is more common than unsuccessful men with great talent. Genius will not; unrewarded genius is almost a proverb.
Education will not; the world is full of educated derelicts.
Persistence, determination alone are omnipotent. "*
— CALVIN COOLIDGE
(1872-1933)
30TH PRESIDENT OF
THE U.S.
(POSTED ALL AROUND
MCDONALD'S
"HAMBURGER U")

Here is that one incredibly simple idea:

FOCUS ON #1

• **First: Focus on Number One.** Mr. Lee said to make a "To Do" list. Write six things you want to do and number them by priority. Be sure each is a goal, or a step toward a goal, not your mission. A goal is specific and attainable. An example of a personal mission might be to become the very best at what you are passionate about. Focus the white hot light of your mind's eye on number one on your list. Work at it as much as you can, every day, until it's accomplished. Then continue to number two and so on. This is what Mr. Schwab paid $25,000 to Mr. Lee for. He said that this plan was largely responsible for turning Schwab's company into one of the largest independent steel producers in the world.

• **Second: Your future goals.** While you're at it, make a six month, one year, and three year goal list. Encourage your spouse do this list as well. Compare notes. You may not be able to get your spouse to participate in this process right away, so put your lists into a notebook and refer to them. Make an appointment with your spouse to review the lists in about six months. For instance, New Years weekend, or on a birthday, or special occasion. I do this on plane flights or long drives with my wife. It is especially rewarding to re-affirm personal ties and "mile markers" toward mutual and individual long-term goals.

• **Third: Your goal attainment habit.** Brian Tracy's other encouragement is to read about things related to your goals for at least thirty minutes every day. Subscribe to related publications. Listen to tapes.

#9: MASTERING YOUR PERSONAL LIFE

Getting Organized is an Everyday Thing

Getting organized is first of all, a state of mind. At some point we finally realize that putting things away where we can readily find them again is the best way. The fog about "messy is easiest" becomes clearly not true. Easier, faster, better, and more mentally satisfying is called being organized.

Getting organized is really about developing good habits. Getting a habit started is hard to do. Like brushing your teeth. After lots of reminding, the habit finally sets in and becomes second nature. The reason New Year Resolutions are dropped so quickly is because we suddenly focus on all we should do. We take on too much. Let's just focus on implementing one habit and let that be all for the year. This one habit is a monthly "To Do" list that you re-do the first of each month and review the first of each week.

Start out simple. Put just a few things on the list that you've been meaning to do for too long a time. Prove to yourself this works and is not the added bother you thought it would be.

Update your "To Do" list at least weekly. Set aside a particular few minutes before or after a regular activity you already do. For example, first thing Saturday after breakfast. At the top of the page write "To Do." Next to it put today's date and the year. Then list down on the page every little thing you want to accomplish as it pops into your mind. Then number the list by priority. Begin working on number one. Don't be distracted by new projects not on your list. Put new jobs on a future "To Do" list. Cross each one off as you accomplish the task or delegate it effectively. Jobs that are on-going may need a status column. What time-line or measurement device will be used? Gather the list in a notebook for a year end review. Be sure at least one "personal goal" is on there all the time in the form of a "To Do" step each week towards that goal.

When you are comfortable with your "To Do" list habit, consider carrying Post-It notes to jot thoughts down on so that you can easily transfer them later to your next "To Do" list.

Time Management Will Set You Free

Time management is really personal goal management. Sadly, less than five percent of us ever write a single goal down. The people who do run the world always have a direction in mind. They get others to help them attain those goals.

Maybe you are following somebody else's goals right now in your daily job? Maybe you are lucky and are part of a team that is also challenged and excited to go toward this goal.

What about the rest of your life? Your family goals? Your personal goals? Time management is not allowing yourself to be easily distracted from your goals.

The best time management idea is to authorize yourself goof-off time. Until you do this you will always feel the pressure even when you are, supposedly relaxing. Your conscience can't really relax, because relaxing isn't on your "To Do" list. So, put it there and give it a priority number along with everything else. If it's a long list, give relaxing another number every so often, identifying the enjoyable thing you want to do. If you don't—don't be surprised when your body gets lethargic, loses oomph, lets you get sick. A multitude of other distractions can also pop up for illogical reasons and take you away from real goals.

When numbering the priority of things to do by importance in a timely way, also consider variety. Don't put all your computer-related jobs together, even though they have "immediate" stamped all over them. Burn-out is another reality you must deal with. When burnout happens, time management goes out the window. It is more important to feel good and have variety. Another suggestion would be to give two or three of the items the same number. Since they have the same importance, you can choose which one you feel like doing as you go along.

"Time is the only little fragment of Eternity that belongs to man; and, like life, it can never be recalled. "
— SAMUEL SMILES
WHO WROTE A 19TH-CENTURY
BESTSELLER SELF HELP
(1812-1904) SCOTTISH-
AMERICAN WRITER

Are you a morning person or an evening person? Plan for the best days and times to do things on your list. Try to get what you dislike doing off your list as soon as possible. Especially the quick ones like phone calls you aren't looking forward to. Anxiety drains mental energy. You will actually gain energy as the not-so-pleasant and not-so-fun jobs are quickly behind you. Don't allow yourself to be sidetracked by trivial thoughts, things, and requests. Stick to your "To Do" list. Start a new "To Do" list for tomorrow and put the interruptions there. With rare exception, if it's not on your list—don't do it.

There are many excellent books and tapes on this subject. The secret is to pick up one habit and work on just that one until it is in your routine. Then go back to your book or list and pick out one more to work on. Don't try to change or create all your habits at once.

Getting Organized is a Matter of Degrees in Improvement

Just a little organization at the beginning of everyday, week, and month brings vast returns. Try a "To Do" list for just one week—you will be surprised. Your "happiness" level will get a big boost, especially as you cross through items when you accomplish them.

Getting organized only seems like extra work before starting. A little extra planning and organizing, thinking about what you want to accomplish, make these steps recoup the most rewards. Here is an example that works in nature, and in science, and in your file drawer.

Let's use pea plants. I remember a science class where we discussed starting with just a white Sweet Pea flower and ultimately got a multi-color bouquet in a very short time. Let's do it the easy way. We need not repeat that experiment since we can take advantage of Gregor Johann Mendel's prior work accomplished in 1866. He was an Austrian botanist and Monk. Just know that a pea seed is predisposed to cast off another color after so many generations. So first we need to have a plan for our bouquet.

We need to plan it on paper as something we want to do, then compare it to everything else we have to do. When do we want this bouquet to arrive in it's beautiful glory? Are there any serious restrictions like a severe winter? What is the need or value? Is it for a craft fair? Does it warrant a greenhouse if you must have it over the holiday season? How big do we want it? "How soon" can be a critical function of organization as you will see. Imagine how this logic applies to almost everything you may want to do.

The goal is at least a bouquet of flowers in less than two months. Notice we are not bogging ourselves down in minutiae at the beginning.

Without organization we plant our seed and maybe water it. A week or so later it has sprouted, produces seeds which fall on the ground. About 10 percent or so take root and grow. This repeats itself with sporadic watering.

With just a little organization to start, dramatic things happen almost right away. First, all the seeds are collected at a pre-planned time. Then a grid of some design is drawn up, a seed is barely pushed under the soil and watered. 95 percent reproduce and we proudly see we have one petunia of a different color. And so it goes, this process is repeated in five short generations we have a beautiful bouquet. Or without planning, something, "kind of nice and a little bit colorful." This is usually followed by a half-hearted promise to do better next time.

This is the working story of your desk, your life, your family, your business, your community. You name it. Any energy that is planned out at the beginning will produce great rewards for you.

Synergy is: Exciting, Healthy and Fun— All Working Together and BOOM!

Independently we each may accomplish a little. However, together, the result is more than the sum of the parts, and the result is synergy. Since we are in the garden, have you noticed how so many plants of the same variety can all be planted the same distance apart? They get exactly the same water and sun. Like corn in a large cornfield, the stalks in the middle area are taller, fuller,and thicker than the ones on the outside edge.

Many things in nature are difficult to explain, but this synergy phenomena seems to work everywhere it's been tried. Your family, your business, everything is affected by the combination of everything else. It is incredibly powerful. Harness this and you will be a true leader. Be careful, synergy works in one direction or the other. In your church or organization, it gets buildings built or it can destroy reputations, or whole countries. Many times it's called perception. It's an unknown quantity. It's that mysterious energy that suddenly wells up and wins, or causes, wars. This is something no one individual can do alone.

Want Change? Practice Doing Things Differently—Chart a Different Course

Will "they" change first, or will you? How do you get people to like you? I remember as a young child looking at my Dad's deep furrowed frowning brow and wondering if I would inherit that! I have the lines today, but the furrows are from the smile lines around the eyes and mouth. How about you? Do you have a ready smile?

"Little things mean a lot. No, little things mean everything."—Harvey Mackay. He also tells us that, "Practice doesn't make perfect — perfect practice makes perfect." You may be doing the same thing poorly over and over again. The fact that you haven't thought about it for awhile is probably proof enough of less than perfect practice.

#10: SUCCESS IS IN THE JOURNEY —PLAN AN INTERESTING ONE

■ ■

Do you have destructive emotions? Are you too argumentative? We are told, we become what we think about the most. I believe it, do you? Success or happiness comes from the positive direction in which we we choose to move. Think positive, you will radiate positively.

Think negative. . .

Planning a Lifetime of Great Rewards

Our rewards will always match our service. Are you in this to do something, or for something to do? You must put in the time to reap the rewards. The daily experience of reaching the goal is most of the success you will feel. Heaven is in the journey. Benchmark where you are today and where you want to be in one year. Don't make improvement too difficult. Better to raise the bar in six weeks, or six months, than to feel that you failed too early. Expect only a few degrees change for each year that you are trying to change.

The idea is for organizational vision. It doesn't get better than this. Your leadership magic is the intensity of your vision. If you can't really get all excited about it, get out! Do the same problems seem to show up everywhere you go? Family relationships? Business relationships? Volunteering in a new field may be a great time to test out some new ways of doing things.

Learn More About Yourself

• To make working play, find what you do easily and with little effort. List out even the little things you like to do: hobbies, gardening; reading.

• Do you have a goal? List out what you are currently working towards. Maybe a job promotion? Winning an award? How about a short term goal, or a mission? Where are you headed? If you do not have a goal in mind you can feel intensely, how about enhancing the quality of your day as a short-term goal? The quality of your life is much more important than just living a long time.

■■■■■■■■■■■■■■■■■■■■

TAKE A FEW MINUTES TO ANALYZE YOUR LIFE AND PEEK INTO YOUR TOMORROWS

Play "This is My Future" with Me

We will analyze your vision, your success and what is important in your life. After your family, what is the other most important thing you want to be accomplishing? If you are not happy, your family isn't either. To have a successful family must first come from within you. Sit back and envision the person you would like to become.

Your Personal Vision

When I first tried to seriously think about my future for more than a few minutes, I drew a complete blank. It was as if my thoughts regarding my future were a complete desert of blah-beige. My very next thought was what a dumb idea this all was anyway. This motivational guy thinks about things differently than I do. He probably can't dance either. I'll just skip this part. Maybe I'll come back to it later, after I've picked up some other ideas further along.

No—no, stop yourself. There is no pressure. This is you about you. Make at least the briefest of outlines. You'll want to save it where you can review it a few months from now.

The other stumbling blocks I threw in front of my way, and I imagined them as big, were: How will I find the time? How will the money come to me personally? Another stumbling block may be, what is a satisfying goal? Then ask, what do your family, friends, customers, clients, and community need that you could provide?

Reach for ideas you haven't dreamed before. Set a direction first, the goal becomes more clear. What are you good at doing? What other strengths do you have? What would it take to get you to commit heart and soul to this vision? Block out twenty minutes of time to dedicate to this and stick with it. Even if you draw a blank for many minutes, relax, nobody is timing you. When you have finally relaxed, ideas will rush forth.

Is this vision for you, also for your family, organization, and your community? If compared to a marriage, it needs to tie together all goal directions in order to work. Like any marriage, there are ups and downs and we work it out. We take time to ask each other about goals as we change and grow ourselves. There's going to be some compromise for the happiness of the whole. Purely selfless people aren't happy people.

What one intermediate goal is most important to you? Write down a mission that is a core belief. Is it "bone deep" within you? Make pledges you will be able to keep, even if these commitments are only short-term at this early stage. You may have a mansion worth of goals. However a modest foundation is a goal you can celebrate, in a reasonable amount of time.

You'll want to gather these sheets into a three-ring binder called, "Goals". Envision your short and long term goals—see them clearly. What the mind can conceive and believe, it can achieve.

> *" The greatest discovery of my generation is that human beings can alter their lives by altering their attitudes of mind. "*
> —WILLIAM JAMES, PSYCHOLOGIST, 1842-1910

> *" A man is what he thinks about all day long. "*
> —RALPH WALDO EMERSON

Positioning Yourself to Begin

Let's see where you are now in the organization of which you are a part. Put yourself and your chosen organization into the new picture. Is there a "fit"? Will others agree? You can lead from anywhere in this organization. What is unique about this organization for you? Write some of your thoughts down as we go along. What must your organization accomplish for you to be aligned and committed to it? You need to inspire yourself somehow. You are the major creator of your environment. You must be motivated in order to help lead others. Pick your challenge once you decide, be ready for the duration. Write it down in your "goals" notebook.

What Are Your Values, How do They Shape Your Priorities for the Future?

What is going to be your comfort level? Are you commander or trustworthy sergeant? Sergeants are very much leaders, too. They are the hands-on, shoulder-to-shoulder teamwork leaders. This really refers to your comfort level. Never get too comfortable. It's very important that you set out numerous clear mile markers for your journey. Celebrate each of them as you reach them.

A NEW DAY —by Dr. Heartsill Wilson

This is the beginning of a new day.
God has given me this day to use as I will.
I can waste it—or use it for good,
But what I do today is important.
Because I am exchanging a day of my life for it!
When tomorrow comes, this day will be done forever,
Leaving in its place something that I have traded for it.
I want it to be
Gain, and not loss;
Good, and not evil
Success and not failure;
In order that I shall not regret the price
That I have paid for it.

Who holds up the world?

It isn't business and it certainly isn't politicians or government. It is humanity's unpaid volunteers. And they do it for their own selfish reasons: family, friends, and community.

ABOUT THE AUTHOR AND SPEAKER

An advertising and direct marketing specialist, Chuck Bennett is a prolific speaker and an author whose last book was a Book of the Month Club selection.

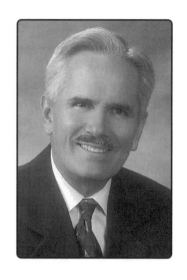

Bennett has been in community leadership positions from his beginnings. Even as a Boy Scout, Chuck rose to Jr. Assistant Scoutmaster on his way to earning Eagle Scout.

Volunteering for the Vietnam draft, Bennett graduated Officer Candidate School. At nineteen was chosen to replace his own trainer and became a Tactical Officer training and graduating new officers as leaders for all branches of the Army. In Vietnam he was an Infantry Platoon Leader and Company Commander until wounded. He then became the Battalion Headquarter Company Commander of over 300 men.

After the service, and earning a BFA degree in Advertising, Bennett started his own business. He has been involved in a variety of nonprofit organizations over the past two decades assuming various positions, chairing committees; as board member, and often as president.

His ideas and examples come from intense study and decades of hands-on experience on various kinds of specialized teams for some of our nations largest corporations ie: IBM, Yamaha, and Carnation, as well as many other national and regional nonprofits.

Known also as "Mr.#1:" for his singular focus on what is most important in reaching a goal, Chuck Bennett has rededicated his life to inspire more volunteer leadership to aid us in taking back responsibilities for our youth, neighborhoods, and communities.

INDEX

V

W